June, 1993

Dear Friends,

Some have called the Tatshenshini the last wild river in the world.

But it's more than a river, more than ancient glacier, rock and wood. It's one of the most spectacular untouched wilderness areas on Earth.

And now, the Government of British Columbia, on behalf of the people of our beautiful province, is proud to keep this area safe forever.

We have permanently protected the entire Tatshenshini-Alsek region in the remote northwest corner of our province -- almost one million hectares -- as a Class A provincial park and nominated it as a World Heritage Site.

The new park will also be the essential link in creating the largest international protected area in the world -- 8.5 million hectares in size -- combining with existing national parks in the United States and the Yukon.

This book beautifully illustrates the unique wildlife, biodiversity, and wilderness recreation values that make the Tat a national and international treasure. As premier of British Columbia, I'm pleased and proud our province has lived up to its global responsibility to keep it that way -- for all Canada, for all the world, for all time.

Mike Harcourt
Premier of British Columbia

Province of
British Columbia

Office of the
Premier

Parliament Buildings
Victoria, British Columbia
V8V 1X4

*"Eventually, all things merge into one,
and a river runs through it. The river was cut
by the world's great flood and runs over rocks
from the basement of time."*

A RIVER RUNS THROUGH IT
From the book by
Norman Maclean
And the film by
Robert Redford

Carr Clifton

TATSHENSHINI

RIVER WILD

To all those who care so much about wilderness
that they are willing to take a stand to ensure
its preservation, and to future generations.
May they, like us, always have the chance
to experience Tatshenshini wild.

John Schnell

WESTCLIFFE
Publisher

SummerWild
Producer

Tatshenshini International gratefully acknowledges all the photographers and writers who donated their work to this project. We would also like to thank those political figures, conservation leaders, members of environmental organizations, and the general public who have worked to keep Tatshenshini wild....forever.

Brian Dechene

John Schnell

John Schnell

Carr Clifton

Rick O'Neill

Carr Clifton

A MOST MAGNIFICENT RIVER
Al Gore

The Tatshenshini-Alsek is one of the most magnificent river systems on earth, flowing through one of the world's most pristine wilderness areas. The region is prime habitat for large mammals, including the grizzly, the rare glacier bear, moose, wolf, mountain goat and Dall sheep, and birds such as the bald eagle, peregrine falcon and trumpeter swan. It is a place of exceptional quality and environmental significance. The Tatshenshini-Alsek features tremendous biological diversity and overwhelming natural beauty, which should be protected and preserved for future generations.

Al Gore

*United States Vice President
Al Gore is committed to a healthy
environment.*

*Indian paintbrush and dwarf fireweed adorn the banks of the Alsek
River. The Brabazon Range dominates the horizon.*

James Katz

A TEST OF GOOD PEOPLE
John Fraser

The ultimate test of a great people is whether, when it comes to choices, they choose wisely. We have a choice with Tatshenshini—to despoil or to conserve.

Those who argue for development say Canada cannot afford to forgo the jobs and economic benefits, even if short-term, that will result from mining. Those arguments are used, and will be used, against most conservation/environmental proposals. They will be used to prevent Canada from saving 12 percent of our natural spaces heritage, an objective endorsed by a unanimous motion in the Canadian House of Commons.

If we had accepted these views without critical examination, we would never have established our national and provincial park systems. We would not have Pacific Rim, South Moresby, Pacific Spirit in Vancouver, the Rouge River in Toronto, and the list could go on. Tatshenshini is magnificent and priceless. Once saved, our children and our children's children will wonder how its exploitation was ever seriously considered.

But first we have to save it. We have a choice, and we shall be measured, as a people, on the wisdom of that choice.

John Fraser is Speaker of the House for the Government of Canada.

The icefield of Walker Glacier flows over precipitous terrain, creating dramatic ice towers known as seracs.

KLUANE
NATIONAL
PARK

DALTON
POST

YUKON

ALASKA   YUKON

B.C.

ALSEK RIVER

TATSHENSHINI RIVER

CANADA
USA

BRITISH COLUMBIA

CANADA
USA

WRANGELL
St. ELIAS
NATIONAL PARK

CHILKAT EAGLE
PRESERVE

HAINES

PROPOSED
TATSHENSHINI
WILDERNESS
PRESERVE

ALASKA

DRY
BAY

ALSEK
LAKE

MT.
FAIRWEATHER

GLACIER BAY
NATIONAL PARK

GLACIER BAY

PACIFIC OCEAN

Graham Osborne

A RIVER FOREVER WILD
Ric Careless

Throughout the eons, the immense tectonic plates of the Earth's crust had drifted slowly atop a mantle of molten, plastic rock. Carried by the currents, they migrated and sometimes collided in imperceptible but relentless fashion. In that part of our planet now called the Gulf of Alaska, two great plates jammed into each other. During millions of years, under enormous pressure, and often heralded by huge quakes, the surface of the land rose. A great range of mountains, including three of the four highest peaks on the continent, was uplifted—the St. Elias.

Over millennia, cool moisture-laden winds blowing off the north Pacific brought heavy snowfall. This accumulated and eventually formed huge glaciers and massive icefields that carved, shaped and sculpted the landscape. In one place, and one place only, along the 400-mile length of the St. Elias Range, the ice breached the mountain barrier, opening a corridor from the subtundra interior to the coastal lowlands. Fed by glacial meltwaters, a powerful river soon flowed in this valley.

Up this great river came the salmon—sockeye and thirty-pound chinook—migrating back in eternal rhythm, year after year, century after century, to the spawning grounds. An astounding abundance of grizzlies and eagles feasted upon them. The bears left their prints on the river sandbars. Wolves, moose and rare, silver-blue glacier

Upper Sediments Creek weaves its way down the valley to join with the Tatshenshini River.

19

Bob Herger

Graham Osborne

Looking west from the Haines Highway, the Alsek Range in mid-June is still smothered in snow.

Icefalls, many several hundred feet high, are abundant in the glacier-plenty watershed.

20

The imposing spires of an icefall dwarf a lone hiker.

bears also came to the water's edge. Far above, in the steep-pitched uplands, mountain goats and Dall sheep grazed.

And so the river raced: broad, wild, incessant. The wilderness around the river was pristine—a green artery threading through a land of lofty peaks and icefields.

Then came the early peoples—Tlingit moving up-river from the coast, the Tuchone down from the interior. Like the bears and the eagles, they too fished for the salmon, and they too thrived. They gave the great river its name: Tatshenshini, meaning Raven's River.

But the wilderness through which Tatshenshini flowed was a raw, young landscape, still changing under the forces of earthquakes, glaciers, mountain uplift and downcutting river erosion. One spring, a few hundred years ago, disaster struck the village at the confluence of the Tatshenshini and the upper Alsek (known to the native people as Kaskawulsh). The villagers heard a thunderous roar and looked up in horror to see a wall of water a half-mile high surging down upon them. A giant ice dam formed on the upper Alsek by the Lowell Glacier, which held back a fifty-mile-long lake, had collapsed, perhaps as a result of the latest great quake. It is said that when it ruptured, a volume of water six times that of the Amazon was released. The forests and soils far up the valley walls were scoured away, leaving a flood line still visible today high above the river. The village site disappeared entirely, lost forever. Now the only reminders of human presence in preflood times are pictographs etched on rocks in a nearby, mid-river island.

Legend has it that only one person survived the flood, and he or she fled to tell the tale of catastrophe. After that, no attempt was made to reestablish a community on the lower Tatshenshini or Alsek. Instead, the indigenous peoples settled in the safer headwaters sites (in the vicinity of today's Yukon-British Columbia border) or at the river's mouth at Dry Bay, Alaska, traveling into Tatshenshini only to fish and hunt. After the calamity that had befallen their people, it came to be revered as the wildest of the wild, the home of the great bear, the place where the mountains quaked, glaciers gave birth to icebergs and an enormous river flowed.

How our planet has changed since that time! In the intervening centuries, intensive settlement and development has altered it almost beyond belief. But up in the northwestern corner of our continent, where British Columbia, Alaska and Yukon converge, the pristine world remains. The Tatshenshini-Alsek still runs pure and free, North America's wildest river. Fed by the world's largest nonpolar icefields, and traversing a spectrum of ecosystems from subarctic to maritime, Tatshenshini-Alsek embodies the essence of wilderness.

Picture a steel-gray, mile-wide river running past mountains that tower 15,000 feet above. Imagine a journey into the Ice Age history of our planet, where glaciers descend to the water's edge: a frozen wall of sapphire-blue, 150 feet high, ten miles wide, calving enormous pinnacles into the river amid thunder and waves.

What a journey the river takes as it rushes 160 miles from source to mouth. Its braided channels are run by returning salmon. Its sandbars record the tracks of both predator and prey. It passes ice falls, peaks and forest, until its glacial waters finally merge with the breakers of the open Pacific.

The Alsek is born of meltwaters flowing fresh from the glaciers on 19,000-foot-high Mt. Logan—Canada's tallest peak. The Tatshenshini begins its journey in British Columbia. Each of these wild waters flow through

An aerial view of the Tatshenshini reveals its braided channels that are forever changing.

Each summer the river is choked with spawning sockeye salmon.

The opaque waters of the Tatshenshini, saturated with glacial till, surge past the Noisy Range.

James Katz

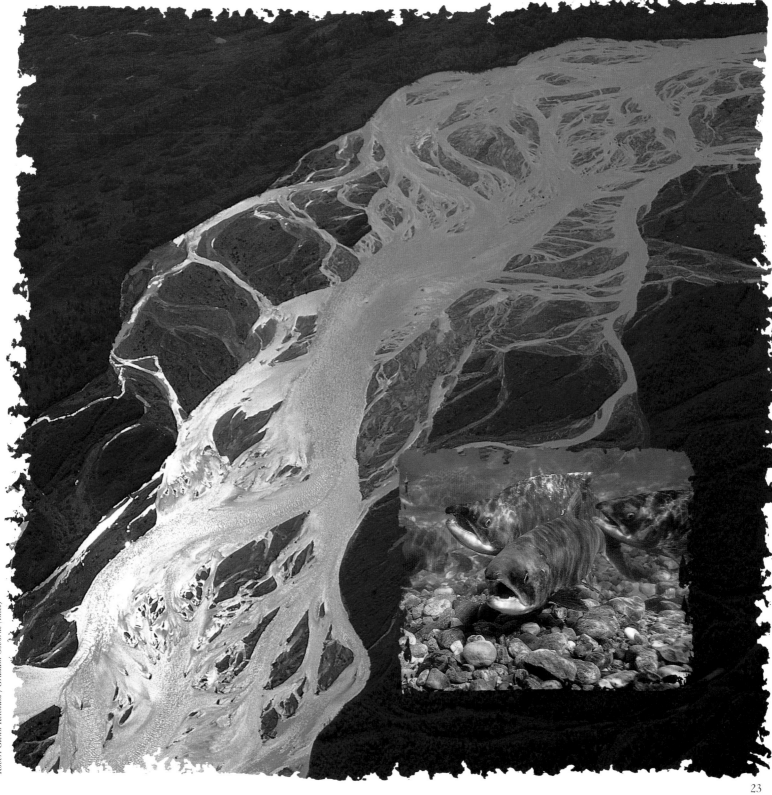

Robert Glenn Ketchum / Graham Osborne (inset)

23

canyon gateways. The upper Alsek boils into Turnback Canyon, one of the toughest stretches of whitewater on the continent. Tatshenshini, milder in character, but spirited nonetheless, follows a green valley important for its grizzly bear populations and its biodiversity. Finally, the two great flows combine and sweep across the international border into the dramatic icefields of Alaska's Glacier Bay National Park.

The vertical relief continues to increase until, to the southeast, 15,000-foot-high Mt. Fairweather reveals its massive majesty. Taking a 90-degree turn through a last range of mountains, the great river flows past pods of stranded icebergs and across the coastal plain to reach the Dry Bay estuary and the Pacific.

How best to label this spectacle? Perhaps "Grand Canyon North" is the most apt comparison, for Tatshenshini-Alsek is a world-class river system. But unlike the Colorado, the Tatshenshini-Alsek flows completely free and pure from headwaters to mouth. Over 2.5 million acres of primeval wilderness, it is the only major drainage on the continent that could be preserved entirely intact.

In 1872, one of the pioneering legends of the world wilderness movement came to this region. That year, John Muir discovered Glacier Bay. He wrote glowingly of the area: "The view is bounded and almost filled by the glorious Fairweather Mountains, the highest among them springing aloft to a height of nearly 16,000 feet, while from base to summit every peak and spire and dividing ridge of the almighty host was spotless white."

Unknown to him, the mountains he saw faced on their opposite flank the adjoining splendor of the Tatshenshini. In subsequent years, Muir's passionate description served as a catalyst for a series of protective actions that together have assembled one of the most important and extensive wildland complexes on the globe: Glacier Bay National Monument—preserved in 1925, made a park in 1980, and extended to encompass the lower Alsek that same year. The Wrangell-St. Elias

Mt. Fairweather, North America's fourth-highest peak at over 15,000 feet in elevation, is an imposing landmark.

24

Icebergs that calve from glaciers into Alsek Lake reveal some fascinating shapes.

Fluting in the mountain walls is caused by erosion from the lateral moraines of glaciers.

25

Generations of grizzlies have prospered in this intact wilderness.

Western columbine (Aquilegia formosa) *is found at moderate elevations on moist mountain slopes, open woodlands and gravel bars.*

was also preserved in 1980. On the Canadian side, the headwaters of the Alsek were protected within Kluane National Park in 1972.

Today, all these parklands are also designated as World Heritage Sites—the highest possible preservation status conferred by the international community.

The only piece of this wilderness puzzle still missing is the British Columbia portion: the Tatshenshini wilderness. Not surprisingly, the World Conservation Union (IUCN) and the United Nations Education and Science and Cultural Organization (UNESCO) have recommended its preservation and nomination for World Heritage status. Tatshenshini's preservation will link together all the adjacent sites to complete the largest international wilderness reserve on Earth: 22 million acres.

Protection of Tatshenshini is in many respects the most critical. If Tatshenshini is preserved, the entire international complex of the St. Elias protected areas will remain safe and self-sustaining. But if development were allowed to penetrate into the center of the wilderness, it would forever endanger not just the Tatshenshini, but surrounding national parks and the wildlife, fisheries and superb landscapes of the entire area.

Such a threat is already dangerously real. Currently, as this book is produced, a Canadian company is proposing to develop a gigantic open-pit copper mine in the very heart of the Tatshenshini wilderness. The project would entail ripping the top off 6,000-foot Windy Craggy Mountain adjacent to the Alsek River; the construction of two huge tailings dams, the highest 350 feet; the laying of 150 miles of pipelines, one to transport slurry copper concentrate, the other fuel oil; and building a road to run alongside and bridge the river. This project would spell the end of wilderness in this now pristine place.

But far worse, the proposed copper mine project would have the potential to poison the Tatshenshini-

27

Large rocks that fall onto glaciers insulate ice below them, creating pedestals as the surrounding ice melts away.

Early morning fog and icebergs on Alsek Lake create a surreal landscape.

Art Wolfe

Bob Herger

28

Mountain goat populations thrive throughout the watershed. Bands of a few dozen animals wander craggy slopes.

Alsek river system with massive acid mine drainage. The ore at Windy Craggy is 40 percent sulphide bearing; exposed to atmospheric oxygen and water vapor through mining, there is a potential to generate vast amounts of sulphuric acid. This could then seep into the bedrock, where it would leach out immense amounts of heavy metal. Should this occur, government agencies in both the United States and Canada say it could devastate the river, as well as the salmon and the exceptional grizzly and eagle populations that have fed upon them for thousands of years.

As Vice President Gore has said, "The development of a huge open-pit copper mine in the midst of one of the world's most pristine regions is an environmental nightmare that threatens the river and every living thing in the region."

Recognizing the threat to Tatshenshini, the environmental movement has rallied in an unprecedented fashion. Over fifty of the leading environmental organizations in the United States and Canada, representing more than 10 million North Americans, have come together to ensure the protection of the Tatshenshini wilderness. One aspect of the campaign is the creation of this book, which is intended to let people know what is at stake.

The writers who have collaborated on this project include conservation leaders and scientists who have long fought for the protection of wild North America. They are joined by political leaders—past and present—from both countries, who feel strongly about the need to keep Tatshenshini wild. The images that help convey the majesty of Tatshenshini are the work of thirty-nine of the best nature, wildlife and outdoor photographers on the continent. These photographers and writers have donated their work in order to help save the continent's wildest river.

In recent years, scientists from around our planet have consistently warned of the need for prompt preservation action. They say that unless we move swiftly to protect biodiversity in large, intact wilderness areas, the extinction of the world's species could become so catastrophic as to threaten global ecological integrity and human survival.

Preservation of the Tatshenshini will join together and complete the largest international biodiversity reserve on the Earth. With the Tatshenshini-Alsek heartland safeguarded, the network of linked preserves in the St. Elias will be extensive enough to ensure the long-term survival of even the top predators: the grizzly and glacier bears, wolf and wolverine, falcons and eagles. It will demonstrate to the world an extraordinary commitment by North Americans to pass on Nature's heritage to future generations.

The effort to protect this astounding river wilderness is one of the great conservation campaigns of our time. For Tatshenshini is indeed North America's wildest river. Those in Canada and the United States who work to save this vast land are leaving a priceless legacy. Tatshenshini is irreplaceable. It must be saved.

Ric Careless is executive director of Tatshenshini Wild in Canada and chairman of the Tatshenshini International network.

Several species of Indian paintbrush (Castilleja), *blooming in a variety of colors, grow in profusion.*

It is hoped that future generations will also be able to enjoy the wilderness beauty of the Tatshenshini.

Liz Mitten Ryan painted Commanding Presence, *a portrait of a grizzly that has no enemies but man.*

Graham Osborne

Ric Careless

Liz Mitten Ryan

Carr Clifton

BIG RIVERS, BIG PEOPLE
Bart Robinson

Big mountains and big rivers attract big-spirited people. Are we surprised, then, that the Tatshenshini, a prodigious river among prodigious mountains, owes its first European descent to a man who had already faced with equal sanguinity the charge of an angry buffalo and the discharge of a flintlock musket? Who had explored the Congo Basin and was later to traverse Africa from the mouth of the Zambezi to the mouth of the Congo? Edward James Glave, a twenty-eight-year-old Englishman, ran the river in 1890 as a member of Frank Leslie's Illustrated Newspaper Alaskan Exploring Expedition. With an Alaskan outfitter named Jack Dalton and a Tlingit shaman named Shank, Glave shot the river in a twenty-foot dugout canoe, drawn by a "keen fascination in traveling through unknown lands," and a desire "to be the first white men to erase from the map the hypothetical and fill up the blank area with the mountains, lakes and rivers which belong to it."

The small party was nearly erased on several occasions. The river, Glave reported, was "the wildest" he had ever seen, and "all of the country was suggestive of violence....Colossal heaps of rock rudely hurled from the mountain heights, the roaring and thundering of the internal forces of glacier and moraine, whole forests laid low by the fury of tempests." Still, his only complaint at trip's end was that the river environs yielded "such an

The Brabazon Range in Alaska's Glacier National Park is the last mountain range the river passes before joining the Pacific Ocean.

The Tatshenshini gorges on hundreds of streams and rivulets, causing it to swell massively as it courses toward the ocean.

Melting snowpack and mountain springs yield clear water, while melting glaciers release glacial till. Eventually, the two blend.

Wolf packs occupy a niche in this intact ecosystem where predator and prey form a natural balance.

Pat O'Hara

Tim Matheson

34

Erwin & Peggy Bauer

incessant display of scenic wild grandeur that it became tiresome."

It is a tribute to the gnarled, remote topography of the Tatshenshini that eighty years passed before it was heard from again. In the early 1970s, the river was redis-covered by a handful of hard-core kayakers—irrepress-ible adrenaline addicts and wilderness connoisseurs, who passed the news of their find on to the larger community of rafting river rats. In August 1976, several stalwarts dropped their inflatables into the river at Dalton Post and whirled away downstream, becoming the first rafters to make the trip and thereby open the river to commercial rafting. American Richard Bangs, founder of Sobek—the world's largest adventure company—was on that journey; today, after eighteen years of world-class river-running,

he still recalls it as, "the most astonishing surprise of my career. We had no idea what we were getting into," he says. "The Tatshenshini is the greatest scenic float trip in the world, the sort of trip that transforms people, and we just wandered smack into the middle of it; no previews, no notions."

Hard on Bang's stern came John and Johnny Mikes, the father and son founders of Canadian River Expeditions, Canada's oldest rafting company. They were looking for rivers to share with clients of their fledg-ling company. It was a quick September run, made with an eye to getting John Jr. back to school, but it was unfor-gettable. "We got it all," says Johnny. "Flawless weather, crisp nights, northern lights, wolves howling, rocks rolling, ice falling—the whole shot. It was gorgeous, and we thought, "Yeah, we could definitely come back here again." And we have, too, every year since 1977. I think of myself as having grown up as a boatman on that river."

Having tested their mettle and discovered magic on the Tatshenshini, such spirits are not likely to fail it in its hour of need, especially now when the proposal to develop an immense copper mine in the heart of the Tatshenshini led to the 1989 campaign to achieve preservation of the river. We don't know what Glave—who belonged to an era when wild scenic grandeur could be taken for granted—would have thought had he lived to see the river challenged, but we have heard full voice from latter-day pioneers. Bangs, like Glave before him, has explored much of the planet's wildness. Placing the Tatshenshini among the greatest of deities in his cosmology of river gods, he says, "Even that the copper mine was ever seriously considered shows an unbelievable ignorance of what the river is and what it represents. When you find a river that moves people the way it does—intellectually, spiritually, sensually—it's a travesty to threaten it. Of the world's thirty-five great rivers that Christian [Kallen] and I included in *River Gods*, the Tatshenshini is the only one that truly runs free from source to sea. There just isn't another like it, anywhere."

For John Mikes Jr., "The Tatshenshini brings all those things together that we think of as wilderness. It's dynamic, a distillation. No matter what your angle is— scenery, wildlife, adventure, biodiversity—the calibre is tops. Through some fluke of geography and history, we have the chance to put this system aside, lock, stock and barrel. It's a little like discovering a new population of some species you thought was extinct, and having the chance to do it right this time."

Big mountains, big rivers. Big spirits, fierce fighters. We need them all.

Bart Robinson

Bart Robinson is editor of Equinox: The Magazine of Canadian Discovery.

Bob Herger

A day from the put-in at Dalton Post, below the whitewater gorges, rafters meander through "Quiet Canyon."

Bob Herger

Bob Herger

The middle section of the Tatshenshini is typified by panoramic vistas and thick brush along the river-bank.

A dip in the icy waters of the river can result in what paddlers call "ice-cream headaches."

37

Graham Osborne

MORE PRECIOUS THAN GOLD
Harvey Locke

Far from civilization, in the most remote corner of British Columbia and through smaller parts of the Yukon and Alaska, runs a powerful, life-giving torrent known as the Tatshenshini. The great river and its valley constitute one of the outstanding wild spaces left on this planet. Together they are the biological heart of one of the world's great wildernesses—the Kluane, Glacier Bay, St. Elias-Wrangell triad. But their future is very much in doubt.

The Tatshenshini is wild North America at its best. No roads penetrate its heartland. The grizzly bear, a wilderness-dependent species, is common throughout the valley. Lewis and Clark wrote of the abundance of these great bears while traveling up the Missouri during their epic exploration of what was then the western wilderness. The grizzly is now gone from the Missouri and from over half of its original home range. But during an eleven-day trip into the Tatshenshini, I saw grizzly tracks every time we pulled the raft ashore. This place is so wild it was marked as "unsurveyed" on maps well into the 1940s.

Most rivers in North America have been treated as sewers, toxic dumps, or sources of cheap energy for industry and water for irrigation. Yet the Tatshenshini, a big river by any standard, is still pure enough to drink. Its waters still run rich with salmon. Bald eagles and golden

Walker Glacier tumbles tons of moraine material into the river.

Bears wander for miles throughout the water-shed, foraging for food and leaving their tracks in soft river mud.

A grizzly meanders the riverbank looking for a place to cross.

Erwin & Peggy Bauer

Bob Herger

40

eagles wheel overhead and lunge for fish. Peregrine falcons slip across the sky and arctic terns hover aggressively above its surging waters. Wolves howl under twilight skies at midnight. The ecosystem functions undisturbed.

I grew up on the lore of the great North American frontier explorers: Lewis and Clark, David Thompson, Alexander MacKenzie. I envied them the chance to see the continent wrapped in its primeval glory. In all my wilderness travels, it wasn't until I was halfway down the Tatshenshini that I felt I had an experience as rich as theirs. The spirit of the great bear is here, and I felt it.

Some might argue that there are other spoils to be had, leading to a network of roads and open-pit mine-sites. But there are already many roads and many mines across North America. There is only one Tatshenshini. When the mines have been exhausted and the wilderness destroyed, what will be left?

Robert Service, the great poet of the north, who watched much of its vast wilderness ravaged by mining, perhaps put it best in his poem, *Spell of the Yukon*.

I wanted the gold and I got it—
Came out with a fortune last fall—
Yet somehow life's not what I thought it,
And somehow the gold isn't all....

There's gold, and it's haunting and haunting;
It's luring me on as of old;
Yet it isn't the gold that I'm wanting
So much as just finding the gold;

It's the great, big, broad land way up yonder,
It's the forests where silence has lease,
It's the beauty that fills me with wonder,
It's the stillness that fills me with peace.

It is my hope and intention that maps of the future will mark the Tatshenshini as "unspoiled"—an international wilderness and wildlife preserve. Surely we can

George Smith

41

Aspen forests provide an ideal understory for other plant life, such as fireweed, to flourish.

42

The prickly wild rose (Rosa acicularis) *can be found in the upper reaches of the Tatshenshini.*

There are beaver all along the Tatshenshini, living in lodges or dens in the riverbank.

bequeath to those who follow a lasting legacy of the Tatshenshini Valley in a wild state. We have taken so much for ourselves.

Harvey Locke is president of Canadian Parks and Wilderness Society.

Kevin Schafer

Erwin & Peggy Bauer

43

Bob Herger

A PERSONAL JOURNEY
Ed Wayburn

The Tatshenshini River is a topic of immense interest for me because of my own personal involvement with its fate.

I had heard of it frequently since the mid-1960s when my wife, Peggy, and I began our long series of annual explorations of Alaska....which are still ongoing. In the early '70s, I flew over the lower Alsek several times and was much impressed by the magnificence of its huge glacial gorge.

But it was not until 1977 that we actually visited the Tatshenshini. In that year, Peggy and I, along with the Sierra Club's Alaska regional conservation coordinator, Jack Hession, and his wife, Mary Kaye, rafted the Tatshenshini from Dalton Post to Dry Bay. At that time, the importance of the Tatshenshini-Alsek river system was largely unknown to the environmental community and to the world. We were able to get some leads on what we were about to experience from Dick Norgaard, who had run the river in 1972. He warned us that in some years the Alsek Glacier would override the Alsek River, making travel very hazardous.

When we were putting together our three-person raft and one rubber kayak at Dalton Post, we were surrounded by a group of Canadians who were fishing for king salmon. An eight-year-old boy was most curious and stayed with us throughout the process.

"Whatcha doin'? Whereya goin'?"

"We're going to float down the river to the ocean."

Just below the O'Connor River confluence, the Tatshenshini takes on another dimension, growing enormously in size due to the added water.

Bob Herger

"Ya can't do that! It's fulla waterfalls...."

"But we're going."

"Then it's curtains oot for you!" said he.

At Dalton Post, the Tatshenshini is small and clear, and it does, indeed, have waterfalls! As the river picks up tributaries, it becomes deep green and grows bigger. Then glacial streams enlarge it much more and turn it gray as it bends into the Alsek and becomes a mile wide—a lively and particularly lovely river to run.

Before Alsek Lake, the river splits: 95 percent of it pours into the left fork, which rushes downhill in a steep gradient into the lake; the remaining water runs to the right, cutting the angle, and meets with the river as it exits the lake. At the last possible moment, we went ashore and, at Jack's insistence, climbed a nunatak to scout that part of the river. The glacier extended all the way across! Had we tried it, it would indeed have been "curtains oot" for us. Instead, we made our way slowly over the much smaller fork to the

Bob Herger

Not far from the put-in at Dalton Post, the heavy snowpack on distant mountains is still evident in mid-June.

The thrills of whitewater rafting are experienced within the first few days of the trip.

The Tatshenshini can be cold and harrowing when rafters encounter whitewater on gray days.

Nick Didlick, Vancouver Sun

James W. Kay

right and reached the river below, well on our way to the Dry Bay takeout.

Our wonderful experience on the river and our realization of its overwhelming beauty caused me to call urgently for inclusion of the lower Alsek in Glacier National Park and Preserve, as part of the 1980 Alaska National Interest Lands Conservation Act. Happily, my recommendation was accepted by the United States Congress.

Ever since, we have enthusiastically supported the ongoing efforts of the range of conservation organizations across the continent to preserve this extraordinary watershed.

Ed Wayburn

Ed Wayburn is vice president of Sierra Club of the United States.

Nick Didlick, Vancouver Sun

48

The level of the water is always in flux, constantly depositing glacial till or thin layers of mud and sand.

As the river widens, it gets shallower, sometimes making dragging necessary.

Below the confluence of the Tatshenshini and the Alsek, winds blowing upriver from the ocean past glaciers create dust storms that can be bitterly cold. On other days, bright, sunny skies are backdrops for beautiful cloud formations.

49

Brian Dechene

A GEOGRAPHY OF SPIRIT
Sally Ranney

On all fours with elbows splayed, nose to mud and eyes squinted against slapping branches, I inched along with my companions through the dense, dripping underbrush near Tats Creek. This was the only way—for miles through tall creekside grasses and tangled trees—to a tiny lake neatly beveled into the ramparts of a small, steep valley.

A peculiar, heavy odor weighted the still, midmorning air, signaling a presence which awakened a response that precedes thought. A profound, primeval respect flooded through me. I rapidly strained for intellectual definition. No time. The senses took over, charging each cell with a long-unused code required for immediate and efficient response. Every hair stood at attention and somehow I could see 360 degrees. I was intruder. I was vulnerable. I was potential prey. I was on fresh grizzly trail in very big and very wild country. For once in my noisy, protected, cement-canyoned life I found myself on the low end of nature's food chain.

Higher. Keep moving. We climbed through a sun-filigreed forest clinging to cliffs above the lake, traversing a creekbed where nature's hieroglyphics were etched in a sandbar: an ancient ritual, eagle eating fish, crossed by later tracks of wolf and grizzly. There was no way to the water's edge, so the view was difficult, brief and privileged: seven rare white trumpeter swans with one black

The midnight sun of summer bathes the mountains in the blush of alpenglow.

51

common loon among them, drifting on tufted waves of cold serpentine green.

I watched, hushed in the presence of ones so wild, so pure of intent and purpose. A stillness of mind softly pushed the prey adrenaline aside and subdued my inner chatter. A vantage point through the trees revealed miles and miles of wildness in which nature has followed its own rhythms each moment of every day in all four seasons, year after year, millenium after millenium. I became deeply calm, surrendering all preconceptions and arrogance to the perfection of it all. Transcending physical existence, buoyed by an overwhelming feeling of timelessness and

Bob Herger

Graham Osborne

52

The stillness, punctuated only by birdsong, is all-pervasive on calm evenings.

Trumpeter swans nest in marshy backwaters and tiny lakes along the upper reaches of the river.

A family of Common loons, which also nest in the area.

A dragonfly rests on a cow parsnip plant (Heracleum lanatum), which is a preferred food of bears.

Mark Hobson

Harvey Locke

53

love, my soul floated with the wind across the lake.

Seven rare, wild, white swans. Seven masters, wisdom keepers of the ancient circle who made decisions for the next seven generations. And only seven great, vast, wild places left on earth. A demonstration of the sacred and a powerful acknowledgment of a greater spiritual power, there was no question in any part of my being that these were the guardians of the Tatshenshini. Only a handful of people have ever been to that lake. Few trumpeter swans are in this great vastness. In the very place, Tats Creek, where some men would tear a hole in the heart of the Tatshenshini for minerals and money, their presence expressed higher purpose and a reminder that love balances the power to destroy.

In twenty years of wilderness conservation work around the globe, I have seen many spectacular places, but I've seldom experienced wildness like the Tatshenshini, a heartland of *22* million acres of wilderness. Like its six sisters—the birthplace of the Amazon and the Okavango of Africa, to name two—it holds the key to humanity's very existence.

These seven places are the Earth's vital organs. Only here in the immense, untrammeled wildness is the essential pulse of Earth's life force strong and in its original state of balance. Here the "Spirit-that-moves-all-things" speaks most powerfully and Nature has unimpeachable rights.

These places hold the voices of wolf and bear, of caribou and great mountain cat, of monkey's scream and serpent's hiss, of fish and eagle, of bones and stones, of feathers and shells, of mice and moles and moose and river

Kevin Schafer

Art Wolfe

song; of wind singing and drill of rain and glacier's calf; of swamp moan and tern crying, termite chewing and beetle mating. They challenge the restraint of the human tribe; they are the protectors of life's genetic archives and the refuge that rekindles primordial fires.

The fate of the Tatshenshini and her sisters is of profound consequence, for they are the geography of spirit, essential to humanity's transformative passage from earthly burdens to the greatest adventure of all, the inner journey to the great beyond.

Sally Ce. G. Ranney

*Sally Ranney is president of
American Wildlands.*

Moose can be found all along the river. Cows and calves must maintain constant vigilance in order to escape their enemies, bears and wolves. Wolves hunt in packs, easily taking a moose calf, often downing a cow. The tracks of both are evident along the riverbank.

Erwin & Peggy Bauer

Art Wolfe

Nick Didlick, Vancouver Sun

SPIRIT OF THE BEAR
Anne Holcroft
Stephen Herrero

Their spirit is present. You know they are never far away. Grizzly bears and black bears abound in the Tatshenshini. Here it is not unusual to watch a sow and cub foraging high up in a subalpine meadow, or a lone male wandering over the gravel flats nipping at locoweed flowers or even battling the rapids of the river to cross its silty gray expanse. Even if you don't see them, you are always aware of their presence: the perfect imprint of a paw in sand that only hours before was undisturbed; trails well worn from centuries of use; droppings red with soapberries, cranberries or devil's club. From these clues, you try to piece together their story. You cannot retire for the night without wondering if you'll rise in the morning to find fresh tracks outside your tent.

Those who are extremely fortunate may catch sight of a glacier bear. This bluish color phase of the black bear is one of the rarest color variants of any large mammal in North America. From a distance, the coat has a silvery, bluish-gray to charcoal-gray hue. Most common along the southeastern Alaskan coast, the glacier bear ranges inland into British Columbia along the lower Tatshenshini River valley. The Tatshenshini region is the only place in Canada where this beautiful animal has been seen. It is not at all difficult, however, to see black bears that are black. The Tatshenshini

In their quest for food, bears crisscross the river, wading channels of all sizes.

Bears stave off any intruders that might steal their food.

Claw marks on trees throughout the watershed are mute evidence of bears.

Spawning sockeye salmon offer high-protein banquets to bears, eagles and other opportunistic feeders.

Bob Herger

Bill Keay

58

teems with these handsome relatives of the glacier bear.

It is the extensive, high-quality habitat along the Tatshenshini River valley that makes this area so attractive to both grizzly and black bears. Maritime air masses penetrate inland to the O'Connor River, a tributary of the Tatshenshini, creating lush vegetation on which the bears feed. The nutritional value of these bear foods is exceptionally high. In spring and summer, bears graze on such plants as horsetail and the celerylike stalks of cow parsnip and angelica that grow in fertile lowland and subalpine meadows. Throughout the gravel flats along the river, grizzly bears use their long claws to dig for the roots of northern hedysarum, a member of the family whose magenta flowers adorn the riverside. As berries ripen on the numerous different shrubs,

bears turn their attention to these energy-rich sources of food. By August, the animals may often be seen on the river banks, rummaging among soapberry bushes, seemingly oblivious to all else.

The only corridor to transect the mighty St. Elias mountains, the Tatshenshini and the Alsek with which it merges is the crucial travel route for salmon returning from the ocean to spawn in the clear-flowing tributary streams. The ever-opportunistic bears take advantage of this high-protein food source. As the salmon migrate up side channels, they may be snatched up by a hungry grizzly bear, eager to add to the fat reserves needed to survive the winter.

The importance of the Tatshenshini to bears is further evidenced by large concentrations of dens excavated by griz-

Phil Timpany

zly bears on the open alpine slopes. Black bears, on the other hand, generally prefer to den in the forest and brush. Insulated by the heavy snowfall, they wait out the long winter in semihibernation.

All of these factors combine to create an exceptional area where grizzly and black bears, including the glacier, coexist and flourish. The vast, untouched wilderness of the Tatshenshini and surrounding national parklands has enabled the wide-ranging grizzly bear to prosper.

As the shadows fade under the bright midnight sky, you can feel the power and the mystery of these great bears. Images come to mind: a young grizzly standing up on its haunches, curious yet intimidating, trying to sense if danger is near; fresh trails through herb meadows where succulent plants have been cropped down to their roots; a riverbank littered with layer upon layer of tracks left by numerous bears; the earth torn up by a grizzly in hot pursuit of an arctic ground squirrel. These all form part of the Tatshenshini experience. Such images confirm that this place is truly wilderness.

Anne Holcroft   *Steve Herrero*

Anne Holcroft is a freelance biologist.   *Stephen Herrero is a leading authority on bear ecology.*

Graham Osborne

60

Art Wolfe

A grizzly dines on salmon using a downed cottonwood tree as a platter.

Dwarf fireweed (Epilobium latifolium), *also called river beauties, are not typical bear food, although the animals may browze on the rich vegetation.*

The glacier bear, a rare, silver-blue color phase of black bear, roams the lower reaches of the river.

61

NATURE'S GARDEN
Heather Hamilton

The sad irony for environmental activists is the almost inevitable urban concentration of our work. Lobbying, working with media, administration—all tend to push those of us who love wilderness into office cubicles in downtown cores. But I escaped! For six weeks in the summer of 1992, I led a scientific expedition into the Tatshenshini. Our goal was to assess and document evidence of the biological wealth of one of the planet's last premier wilderness areas.

Guided by an expert botanical specialist, Dr. George Douglas, our group became addicted field botanists. Hikes took much longer—every few yards, it seemed, we encountered a fascinating new plant or flower that demanded attention and challenged us to identify it. Serious discussion usually ensued about the presence or absence of one or another characteristic and the exact identification of species. Were the leaves on this plant hirsute or glabrous (hairy or bald)? Did this grass have a drooping panicle or an awnless glume? Photos were taken from every angle and field guides were eagerly rooted out of pockets. Some unfortunate flowers were pulled up, sacrificed to the evening campfire tutorials for positive identification later. Here we learned to twist our tongues around names like *Boschniakia rossica*, a saprophytic plant that grows on alder and looks like an elongated pine cone, or *Saxifraga oppositifolia*, the beautiful purple

Alpine forget-me-nots (Myosotis alpestris) *and mountain buttercups* (Ranunculus eschscholtzii) *are prolific in high alpine meadows.*

A *natural garden of several species of* Indian *paintbrush and river beauties blanket the riverbank.*

Wild geraniums and paintbrush are marvellous examples of the intricate beauty of wildflowers.

Carr Clifton

mountain saxifrage.

Early on in our trip, at a place called Sediments Creek, we came across the unusual and quite appropriately named chocolate lily almost hidden among tall grasses. A few miles downstream, at the confluence of the O'Connor and the Tatshenshini, magenta carpets of fireweed bordered the river. Still farther downstream, where dozens of glaciers stretch their fingers towards the river, Indian paintbrush (or *Castilleja*, its musical botanical name) bloomed in such profusion that we were reminded of cultivated rockeries and English country gardens. The flowers were crimson, scarlet, salmon, tangerine and pale butter yellow.

In the mountains and valleys bordering the river, we found towering eight-foot-tall cow parsnip, thorny devil's club in abundance, and several species of *Hedysarum*, or

James Katz

Art Wolfe

Kevin Schafer

sweet vetch, all dietary staples of grizzly and black bear. In the high alpine, we discovered delicate, minute, alpine tundra beauties, which for me invoked nostalgia for my High Arctic field days. At the confluence of the two great rivers, the Alsek and the Tatshenshini, we encountered, to our delight, a plant that had not changed in over a million years. The moonwort is not a relic but a happy survivor that still thrives in this great intact wilderness.

For the field team, the end result of all our studious activity was a deepening sense of wonder at the endless variety of flora we were finding. We soon came to appreciate that while grizzly bears, dynamic rivers and towering, glacier-cloaked mountains may be the most acclaimed and recognized attributes of the Tatshenshini, without doubt its most overlooked and underrated charm rests with the flowers. Hidden among the mountains, fringing the rivers, and nurturing the bears and other animals is a vast profusion of plants patiently waiting to be discovered. From the frugal alpine tundra to lush coastal gardens, a floral coat of many colors clothes the Tatshenshini.

Heather Hamilton

Heather Hamilton is conservation director for the Sierra Club of Canada.

Dwarf dogwood (Cornus canadensis) *is a tiny plant that forms a groundcover under the protection of aspen trees.*

Bouquets of alpine forget-me-nots, columbines, paintbrushes, wild geraniums and river beauties brighten the riverbank even on dull days.

Bill Keay

A SPECTACLE OF EAGLES
Peter Enticknap

From the tiny rufous hummingbird to the enormous golden eagle, the Tatshenshini is blessed by the bird world. Over 180 species, representing some twenty-six different feathered families, frequent the river valley during spring and summer.

The memories a birder might take away from a rafting adventure on the Tatshenshini are many and varied: the drumming of a ruffed grouse; the high-pitched, electronic sound of a varied thrush's song; the beautifully haunting song of a hermit thrush; a willow ptarmigan's cautious departure; a semipalmated plover feigning a broken wing to distract unwelcome visitors from its nest; and parasitic jaegers, avian pirates relentlessly harrassing mew gulls at Alsek Lake.

One of the sweetest experiences, if your trip occurs early in the season, during the seemingly endless days when the alpenglow of evening is the darkest it gets, is to be lulled to sleep at midnight by the melodies of the golden-crowned sparrow, the Swainson's thrush, the warbling vireo and the northern waterthrush—all blending into nature's orchestral symphony only inches above your tent!

But to all bird-lovers, the constant presence of bald eagles is a marvellous sight. Clusters of a half-dozen or more eagles sitting in the limbs of trees at water's edge or on the riverbars are frequently seen. Typically, on the trip

Majestic bald eagles are constant companions during a journey down the river.

During the early winter salmon run on the Chilkat River, part of the Tatshenshini Triangle, thousands of bald eagles congregate to feed on the spawning fish.

Pat O'Hara

George Figdor

from Dalton Post to Dry Bay, in excess of a hundred or more eagles will be sighted.

An eagle is a remarkable creature. Its vision is eight times that of humans, enabling it to see a rabbit at two miles. It can dive at speeds of up to 200 miles per hour, striking prey with the force of a bullet. Fish, waterfowl and small mammals are its primary food. Bald eagles become sexually mature in five to six years, when they develop their characteristic white head. Subadults, which are common on the Tatshenshini and in the Chilkat Valley, adjoining the Tatshenshini Triangle, are easily distinguished by their marbled brown and white plumage.

Eagle nests are usually found within 200 yards of a body of water in large, old-growth trees. A clear flight path to open water ensures hunting success. Active nests are eight feet in diameter. They can weigh a ton or more and are added to each year.

Some 100,000 bald eagles once populated the continental United States, but loss of habitat, mortality due to DDT, and indiscriminate hunting reduced their numbers to 400 nesting pairs by the mid-1960s. Today in the Lower 48, a multimillion-dollar restoration program using relocated eagles from Alaska has led to numbers climbing to 2,600 nesting pairs. Despite these gains, thousands of eagles are still killed each year by poisoning and illegal hunting. In Alaska, it is estimated that half of the state's 30,000 northern bald eagles (*Haliaeetus leucocephalus Alascanus*) live in southeast Alaska, where the best habitat and food sources—especially salmon—occur.

Eagles in this state have also been persecuted.

Bill Keay

Between 1917 and 1953, a bounty was offered by the Alaska Territorial Legislature. More than 128,000 eagles were killed for just two dollars a bird. When Alaska became the forty-ninth state of the United States, bald eagles were protected by the National Bald Eagle Act of 1940.

However, it was only after two decades of often bitter and violent controversy over mining and logging that true protection finally came for these superb birds on the Chilkat River, with the formation of the Alaska Chilkat Bald Eagle Preserve, near Haines, Alaska, in 1982. Almost the entire population of Tatshenshini bald eagles gathers at this river in the late fall to overwinter. These are transboundary birds with dual "citizenship": summering in Canada and going to southeast Alaska for the winter! Rafters headed for the Tatshenshini from Haines enjoy a firsthand opportunity to experience this preserve on their way to the put-in.

Thousands of bald eagles congregate here in the famed Valley of the Eagles on the Chilkat, making it one of North America's premier wildlife spectacles. Attracted by a late run of chum salmon, eagles come from Glacier Bay National Park, the Tatshenshini wilderness and as far away as Washington State for the abundant feast. The 4,000 birds that gather here are the largest concentration of eagles in the world.

For this amazing avian odyssey to continue, as well as visions of graceful terns hovering, glorious trumpeter swans nesting, red-breasted mergansers sunning on floating logs and horned larks flitting about in subalpine meadows, the health of the incredible Tatshenshini wilderness must remain intact.

Peter Enticknap is vice chairman of Tatshenshini International.

Erwin & Peggy Bauer

Ptarmigan are high-alpine dwellers whose plumage changes color from mottled brown to white when winter comes.

Semipalmated plovers nest on gravel bars, where their eggs are camouflaged among the rocks and pebbles. An adult bird will feign a broken wing when an intruder comes near the nest.

73

A BIODIVERSITY KEYSTONE
Monte Hummel

A glance at the range map of North America's most spectacular wildlife species—top predators such as the grizzly bear, black bear, wolf, cougar and wolverine—reveals a tide of extermination that has pressed these "super species" to retreat farther into the north and west. And there, in the heart of the continent's wildest, most remote remaining habitat, lies the Tatshenshini-Alsek watershed. The Tatshenshini Triangle is nestled like a keystone in a medieval arch; with adjacent protected wilderness areas—Alaska's Wrangell-St. Elias and Glacier Bay national parks, and Yukon's Kluane National Park—it completes the largest international biological diversity reserve on our planet.

The sheer size of the Tatshenshini wilderness and adjoining areas is crucial. For example, conservation biologists working with World Wildlife Fund have estimated that the area required to sustain a minimum viable population of grizzly bears is 19,650 square miles, and it is 26,650 square miles for wolverine. Since very few areas this large remain in the world, it is not surprising that few wild populations of these space-demanding top predators have held on. But when you preserve the Tatshenshini heartland and thereby link together already protected areas, there is the potential for a wilderness preserve of nearly 42,400 square miles—truly a biodiversity reserve of global significance and perhaps the only place in Canada where the long-term

There are numerous herds of mountain goats, sure-footed animals that can survive the harsh conditions of winter here.

A bull moose sheds the velvet from its antlers during the summer, prior to the fall rutting season.

Wolves will prey on moose, but it is unlikely a wolf pack would tackle a healthy bull.

The only winter range in British Columbia for Dall sheep is in the upper reaches of the Tatshenshini, where the snowpack can be blown clear, allowing the animals to browse.

Erwin & Peggy Bauer

Erwin & Peggy Bauer

survival of the grizzly is assured. Preservation of the Tatshenshini—the unprotected core of this area and its vital grizzly habitat—is essential.

Conservationists now have a rule of thumb: make a protected area large enough to accommodate a viable population of the top predators, and you more or less capture everything else in the ecosystem. This would include, for example, the top predators' prey species, such as moose and caribou, the plants upon which they and many other species depend, and the soil and microorganisms which account for the fundamental richness of the system as a whole. Therefore, managing for large carnivores is really managing for ecosystems. But the key is big wilderness, and that, above all, is what protecting the Tatshenshini area provides.

Traveling the Tatshenshini brings this general argument alive. Sandbars of the river are crowded with tracks of moose, wolf and grizzly bear. Dall sheep wander the rugged uplands. The rare glacier bear, a bluish-silver phase of the black bear, is found only here, along with regionally rare mammals such as the collared pica and tundra shrew. Even seals and sea lions have been observed swimming up the Alsek, some thirty miles into Canada and the Tatshenshini wilderness area!

James Katz

Avian top predators, such as bald and golden eagles, peregrine and gyrfalcons, testify to the health of the system below them on the food chain as well. For the eagle, of course, this means a thriving salmon run, which Tatshenshini provides. Trumpeter swans, nationally classified in Canada as "vulnerable," and regionally rare species, such as the Hudsonian godwit, stage and nest in the area's remote shorelines, bays and wetlands.

Such outstanding wildlife values are attributable to more enduring features of the landscape. The Tatshenshini is essentially the only low-elevation corridor through the St. Elias Mountain Range. As such, it is an extremely important wildlife migration corridor. From a biodiversity standpoint, the Tatshenshini and adjoining protected areas serve as home for a full range of creatures and habitats, from sea level to elevations exceeding 19,000 feet, and from the outer west coast to the interior subtundra. The Tatshenshini and Alsek river valleys are particularly productive because the vegetation feasts on moist air penetrating far inland from the coast. But perhaps most important of all, since the headwaters are locked off by a canyon and a formidable range of mountains, the heartland of British Columbia's Tatshenshini has remained roadless and totally intact. This is a remarkable fact when compared to the lower United States, where the farthest point from a road is only seventeen miles.

The wildlife species of the Tatshenshini, striking as they are in their own right, really serve as a symbol of something more fundamental. The bears, moose, eagles, swans, salmon and plants tell us something more important about the nature of the land itself. The Tatshenshini wilderness is a scarce example of what Aldo Leopold called the "Theatre of Evolution." It is still wild. May it always be.

Monte Hummel is president of World Wildlife Canada.

Bear tracks lead to Walker Glacier, where grizzlies have been seen wandering across the icefields.

The wolverine is another predator that frequents the watershed, but it is seldom seen.

Spent salmon, in the last phase of life after spawning, are a food source for dozens of animals above them in the food chain.

79

Bart Henderson

PADDLING TURNBACK
Ken Madsen

The Alsek River is thick with glacial silt. It hisses and pops against the side of my kayak. Icy fingers of Tweedsmuir Glacier reach through dark hills of terminal moraine. The river, squeezed between Turnback Canyon's rock walls, rises like a breaching grey whale and disappears in a swirl of white.

The Alsek is the finale of the "Tatshenshini Wilderness Quest," a series of kayaking expeditions on the three rivers that are the lifeblood of the wildest land in North America. We've already paddled the Chilkat and Tatshenshini rivers. Turnback Canyon is the final challenge on the quest.

Jody Schick and Ian Pineau wait downstream. I'm nervous about the surging whitewater at the bottom of the rapid, specifically the wave that swallowed Jody's red kayak like a ripe cherry, spitting out the seed upside-down. Jody is young and confident enough to be unconcerned with minor details like mortality. Not me. I remember the words of Walt Blackadar, the first person to paddle Turnback Canyon in 1972.

This has been a day! I want any kayaker to read my words well! The Alsek gorge is upaddleable! Unbelievable....
I'm not coming back. Not for $50,000; not for all the tea in China. Read my words well and don't be a fool. It's unpaddleable.

A kayaker sets up to run Turnback Canyon, one of the wildest stretches of whitewater on the continent.

I understand Blackadar's feelings. In the two decades following his adventure, only three other groups have successfully paddled Turnback Canyon. In 1981, a young French kayaker drowned during an aborted attempt at the "first European descent" of the canyon.

The mystique of Turnback is more than its powerful whitewater. It is a product of the land itself. I have paddled extensively on several continents, including renowned rivers such as the Colorado's Grand Canyon and the Nahanni. These splendid streams flow through stunning landscapes, but only on the Tatshenshini and Alsek rivers have I felt my nerves tingle with such life.

I've paddled the Tatshenshini and the Alsek a half dozen times—following the only valleys that pierce the St. Elias Mountains from the interior to the Pacific. I've made first descents of the Bates River and Tats Creek, exciting streams that cascade out of the high country.

Other mysterious and unpaddled rivers invite exploration, including the O'Connor and the Tkope.

You don't need to be submerged in a violent rapid to feel this land's magic. You experience it in the cold of glacier ice under your boots, in the sound of wind buffeting your tent, in the sight of a calving iceberg. Wherever I travel in this wilderness, I feel a sense of insignificance, a sense that I don't have power over the landscape. It's a good feeling, one that I try to hold onto when I return to "civilization."

The crux of Turnback Canyon is a stretch of whitewater that Blackadar named "*Hair*—the worst foamy rapids a kayaker can imagine." His description is accurate. I slide past a turbulent boil and plunge through an ominous narrowing. A wave breaks over my head and I submarine downstream. I pop to the surface, relieved to be under control again as the powerful rapid tosses me

Ken Madsen

Bob Herger

Challenging the rapids, a paddler must rely on skill, strength and luck.

The more open, gentler waters of the upper Tatshenshini, between Sediments Creek and O'Connor River, offer a scenic ride.

83

*A kayaker cautiously approaches an active,
potentially dangerous, calving wall of ice.*

*Smaller icebergs create interesting paddling,
but caution is necessary in case winds close off
access channels.*

Ken Madsen

84

into an eddy like a piece of driftwood.

Several hours and many rapids later, my companions and I squirt through the final constriction in the canyon. A bald eagle circles above the towering rock walls. Around the next corner, a sow grizzly with a pair of cubs watches the bright splotches of color that are our kayaks. We have survived what Blackadar called the "unpaddleable" canyon.

As we float towards the Pacific, Turnback becomes a jumbled memory of swirling water and brooding rock walls. The whitewater and adrenaline are no longer of paramount importance. The images clearly etched in my mind are of the eagle and the bears, symbols of the strength and richness of this immense wilderness.

Ken Madsen

Ken Madsen is a writer, photographer, outdoor educator and kayaker.

Art Wolfe

Bob Herger

85

Michael Down

PEAK EXPERIENCE
Pat Morrow

The Tatshenshini and Alsek river drainages receive their nourishment from the mighty icefields of the Wrangell-St. Elias mountain ranges. Superlatives lauding the physical attributes of the St. Elias Mountains roll easily off the tongue. Having climbed the highest peaks on each of the seven continents, I believe I can say this mountain region is among the world's most breathtaking, comparable in scale and purity to the Himalayas and Antarctica. The 22-million-acre wilderness domain that sprawls from the Copper River in south-central Alaska, through western Yukon Territory and northwestern British Columbia, and down to Glacier Bay in the United States contains the largest concentration of high peaks in North America. Canada's highest and the continent's second-highest summit, the massive Mt. Logan, stands at 19,545 feet, in supreme isolation at the heart of it all. Separated from other peaks by vast expanses of glaciers such as the Hubbard and the Seward, Logan has the greatest base circumference of any mountain on earth.

This international wilderness area boasts the largest ice cap outside the polar regions. The heavy accumulation of glacial ice accounts not only for the moist climate of the coastal areas on its southeastern fringes, but generates weather patterns from the Gulf of Alaska that affect the rest of North America.

The St. Elias Range contains the highest coastal

The mountains of the Wrangell-St. Elias Range offer some of the most spectacular climbing opportunities in the world.

Summer hikers and mountaineers enjoy terrain that is carpeted with many species of lupine and heather. Once alpine meadows are won, magnificent vistas are the reward.

John Schnell

Mark Hobson

mountains in the world; in some cases they exceed the Himalayas in vertical relief. Emanating from the central ice cap, some of the world's longest glaciers flow in a slow, sinuous pattern toward tidewater on the Pacific Ocean. Within thirty miles of the Pacific Ocean, Mt. St. Elias rears up, the third-highest peak on the continent at 18,008 feet. Farther down the map, just south of the Tatshenshini-Alsek rivers on the Alaska-British Columbia border, Mt. Fairweather rises to 15,300 feet, the fourth-highest peak in North America. And the St. Elias Mountains are so young, they are still in uplift.

Climbers were initially lured to this northwestern part of the North American cordillera by the chance to be the first to explore the vast expanse of snow and ice and tread on their virgin summits. In 1867, one of the more colorful expeditions arrived on the beach near the toe of the Malaspina Glacier. Traveling all the way from Italy, the Duke of Abruzzi had his sights set on the first ascent of Mt. St. Elias. Accompanying the Duke was his entourage of Italian climbing guides, the great mountain photographer, Vittorio Sella (one of the glaciers near Mt. Logan carries his family name), and several hired American porters. The porters were needed to drag the 700-pound sledge that contained, in addition to the expedition's food, equipment and supplies, a brass bed for their patrician leader.

In 1925, a joint Canadian-American team led by A. H. MacCarthy was launched to climb the more remote Mt. Logan. So complicated were the logistics, and so well executed, that Captain Noel, the documentarian of Mallory and Irvine's attempts on Mt. Everest, held them up as a standard on which expeditions to any part of the globe could be based. In early spring, an advance team ferried supplies by dogsled to the mountain's base ahead of the main team. Struggling against the characteristically severe subarctic elements—temperatures plunging below -40° F and gale-force winds exceeding sixty miles per hour—and the debilitating effects of high altitude, the indomitable team used primitive equipment and clothing

Art Wolfe

to gain the summit without any loss to life or limb.

In the intervening years, the range has experienced sporadic incursions by climbers, surveyors and scientists. However, with popular climbing destinations becoming overcrowded in other parts of the world, the number of climbers and skiers coming to the Wrangell-St. Elias increases every year. Predictably, most of them are drawn to the slopes of Mt. Logan, simply because it is the highest feature in the range. However, there are also the adventuresome parties who are looking for the quality of personal experience that their predecessors sought. Extremely difficult routes are established on unclimbed faces and ridges of previously climbed mountains. So vast is the range that many of these climbs to this day are first ascents on unnamed peaks.

Pat Morrow

Pat Morrow is a writer, photographer, filmmaker and mountaineer.

Robert Glenn Ketchum

In early summer, alpine meadows are still dotted with snow-rimmed ponds.

Ice tunnels on Walker Glacier, created by flowing water, will vanish by the next summer.

A dusting of pink on the mountain range behind the glacier locks in a memory that will last for a lifetime.

91

Michael Down

A FAIRWEATHER VIEW
Michael Down

Whether you take in the view while floating in the pull of the river's relentless currents or gazing out from the thick brush at its edge, the Tatshenshini Valley seems as wide as the imagination. It's as if Mother Earth herself had opened her arms wide to hold its lush tangle of scrubby forest and the many creatures that make this place home.

But there is another view of the Tatshenshini, and it is a very different one. It can only be had from the tops of the highest mountains that rise like sentinels standing guard over the river. From these lofty points, the expansive valley narrows down to a thin ribbon of green, like a vein throbbing with life, piercing the frozen glacial vastness of this wild and remote land.

One bracing day in June 1989, we were treated to such a view from the summit of Mt. Fairweather, which soars 15,300 feet right off the North Pacific coast, making it British Columbia's highest mountain. An icy wind shrieked in our ears like wicked laughter; gloveless hands fumbling with cameras went stiff and numb in seconds. But the usually sullen skies of the Alaskan gulf had granted us a reprieve and opened up to reveal a flawless blue sky. To the west, some 15,000 feet directly below, we could almost make out the surf of waves breaking on the beach. To the distant north, cutting a sinuous, emerald path through a maze of pyramidal mountains, ran the

A climber struggles over a snowy peak. These snows, which feed glaciers that melt into streams and eventually rivers, may take hundreds—or even thousands—of years to reach the valley floor.

Tatshenshini.

After five days of harrowing and arduous climbing to reach the summit, we were rewarded with a view limited only by the curve of the distant horizon. Despite the bitter wind, those breathtaking moments afforded a time to reflect and catch a glimpse of the purity, simplicity and beauty of life, which usually gets lost in the day-to-day scrabble for a living.

For the most part, however, climbing in these mountains is much less romantic. Much time is spent struggling with fear and fatigue, expending massive physical effort carrying brutally heavy packs over terrifyingly steep and exposed terrain, where an avalanche might threaten from above or a momentary loss of concentration might mean a fatal slip into the abyss below. Our route on Fairweather, up the previously unclimbed southeast ridge, was classically typical of the St. Elias Mountains— snaking up sharply faceted, knife-edge ridges and picking a precarious route along the tortured, convoluted edges of wind-whipped cornices.

For every day of action, there's one of inaction, and that is another kind of tension one has to deal with on these climbs. Time yawns away into endless boredom, during stormbound days spent in numbing lethargy within the coffinlike confines of a tiny tent. The body aches for movement, while the mind becomes dazed from lack of focus and the incessant slapping of the nylon tent as it thrashes violently in the wind.

And then there are those special moments woven into a climb that make all the efforts worthwhile; those moments of magic where one is filled with peace and ease and contentment with oneself and the world around—like our time on the summit of Mt. Fairweather.

Technical mountaineering is a high-risk game. Every action must be evaluated for its potentially fatal consequences, and with that intensity of concentration comes an immediate awareness of the fragility and preciousness

Bob Herger

The sun sets first in the valleys, leaving the peak of Fairweather crowned with a warm glow.

Hikes to high alpine yield powerful insights into the heart of a vast mountain range.

Tight cushions of moss campion (Silene acaulis) await visitors to alpine meadows.

Mike Beedell

Kevin Schafer

95

of life—not just of our own lives, but of all life. Perched on the summit, surrounded by a frozen and lifeless landscape of dark rock and glacial ice, that distant view of the verdant Tatshenshini makes it clear what a fragile oasis thrives there. From the top, we made prayers that the valley be left undisturbed to thrive in its own time-honored way.

Michael Down

Michael Down is one of Canada's most accomplished mountaineers.

Michael Down

Michael Down

Climbing expeditions to this rugged, remote landscape must be expertly planned and skillfully executed.

A climber returns after an ascent of the southeast ridge of Mt. Fairweather. Dry Bay, Alaska and the open Pacific stretch out below.

Jim Haberl

97

Jim Katz

THE WILDEST RIVER
Tom Cassidy

The history of river conservation tells the story of endangered places. Some magnificent river areas drowned behind dams include the Tuolumne's Hetch Hetchy Valley, the Colorado's Glen Canyon, and the Quebec rivers lost to the James Bay project. Rivers such as the Columbia-Snake, the St. Lawrence and the Mississippi cry out for restoration from the effects of dams, diversions, development and channelization. Ironically, acid mine drainage, the great threat to the Tatshenshini-Alsek, poisons more miles of river in the United States than are protected in the National Wild and Scenic Rivers system. Even the headwaters of Norman Maclean's beloved Big Blackfoot River, portrayed in the film *A River Runs Through It*, are poisoned by acid mine drainage from abandoned mines.

Preservation of the Tatshenshini-Alsek river system is widely recognized as a top-priority river conservation issue in North America.

Several years ago, my wife, Joy, and I were immensely impressed by the power and magnificence of the river. At Dalton Post, where our trip began, the Tatshenshini is a modest-sized river that merely hints at its downstream grandeur. Tracks of grizzly, wolf and moose, and bald eagles feasting on spawned-out salmon, signal the entrance to wilderness. Voyaging downstream, each day the river grows larger, the country wilder, and the memo-

Huge rocks, part of glacial debris, are either floated down on melting ice or hurled down by earthquakes.

ries of permanent human presence more distant. The enormous expanse of wilderness everywhere, in every direction, is astounding.

If we are fortunate, each of us during our lives will get to experience places of overwhelming power and majesty. The confluence of the Tatshenshini and Alsek is such a place. Two massive rivers; more than twenty glaciers streaming blue and white between jagged, steep mountains; alpenglow; wildflowers; and evidence of abundant wildlife combine in a symphony of magnificent beauty.

At the confluence, the river has grown to become a huge, glacial-braided flow, more than a mile wide, more akin to a fast-running ocean than a river. Below the confluence, the river takes on a new dimension as it becomes the Ice Age river, cutting through the largest nonpolar ice fields on earth. In the shadow of Mt. Fairweather, in the middle of Alsek Lake, we marvel at the thunderous crack of icebergs calving from glaciers into the river. Then we alternately laugh with innocent joy and respect the majesty of silence as we float among surreal blue sculptures of river icebergs.

Today, the headwaters and lower reaches of the Alsek River are protected within Kluane National Park in Canada and Glacier Bay National Park in the United States. The global significance of the resources possessed by these jewels of the two nations' national park systems has led to their designation as World Heritage Sites. But the biological diversity of Glacier Bay and Kluane depends on the protection of the ecological core of the Tatshenshini-Alsek river system. This protection is important to preserve not only the critical habitat of the rivers themselves, but also to protect a "ribbon of green" for wildlife and plant species between the Gulf of Alaska and the Yukon interior.

American Rivers has identified the Tatshenshini-Alsek river system as one of America's ten most endangered rivers for several years. In 1992, Vice President Al Gore (then a United States senator), announced the

Profuse on gravel bars, yellow dryas (Dryas drummondii) *evolve from a tight conical yellow flower into a fluffy seedhead.*

Johnny Mikes

Rafters float the Alsek River below Kluane National Park, near the confluence with Bates River and above Turnback Canyon.

Survivors of avalanches, strips of aspen rim hillsides.

Art Wolfe

Drying glacial silt creates fascinating designs in the riverbank.

Rocks rounded by bowling down miles of rushing water form picturesque mosaics.

The river is a floodplain constantly in flux. Logs and other debris create anchors for soil that encourages the growth of dwarf fireweed and willows.

introduction of legislation to protect the Tatshenshini-Alsek river watershed as a World Heritage Site at the American Rivers "Endangered Rivers" press conference. Every evaluation of the proposed mine development demonstrates that it is, as the vice president stated, "an environmental nightmare waiting to happen."

In 1980, the historic Alaska Lands Act included the United States portion of the Alsek River in an expanded Glacier National Park because of the wilderness, wildlife and recreational values. The United States Congress requested that the secretary of the interior enter into cooperative agreements with Canada to protect the entire Alsek River watershed. Such a vision of international cooperation was not acted upon in the 1980s; however, conservationists across the continent are hopeful that the Clinton-Gore Administration will seize upon Congress's long-delayed request and the vice president's 1992 legislative initiative.

Canada and the United States now enjoy the rare and historic opportunity of demonstrating to the world the importance and urgency of protecting large river ecosystems. Preservation of the Tatshenshini Triangle will result in the protection of a rare species: a wild river ecosystem intact from its headwaters to the ocean.

The protection of the Tatshenshini-Alsek river system, and its surrounding wild lands, is the essence of river conservation. Joy and I will not be able to share with our young sons the grandeur of a pristine wild river in Glen Canyon or Hetch Hetchy. The struggle to keep those rivers wild was lost. However, if our efforts to preserve the Tatshenshini-Alsek river system are successful, then all of us—and our children—will be able to enjoy the wilderness waters of the wild Tatshenshini.

Tom Cassidy

Tom Cassidy is general counsel for American Rivers.

Brian Dechenes

Art Wolfe

SOMETHING ABOUT A RIVER
Brock Evans

There is something about a river—a great wild river—
that reaches deep into me, tugs at the inner most recesses of
my own soul. I have felt this magic and power on some of
America's great western rivers: the Snake, the John Day, the
Colorado, the Missouri. I cannot explain exactly that peculiar
combination of senses and action that come together to
touch me in this way. It is something more than just the
grand play of light and shadow on rock cliffs, something
beyond the distant roar of the rapids around the next bend,
the lazy gyre of a hawk circling high up in the afternoon
breeze. It is insistent and incessant, it tugs and pulls at me,
bearing me on and on, down around the next bend, to the
next place. Different from the grand, wild, mountain scenes
of the climbing days of my youth, it is the sense that the
river itself is alive, has motion, purpose, power, that attracts
me so.

And of all the rivers I have known that have touched
me in this way, the Tatshenshini is surely the greatest, the
grandest, the wildest—at the top of the list of the greatest
remaining free-flowing rivers on this planet. These were the
emotions that swept through me two years ago, on about the
sixth or seventh day on the river. Starting when it was only a
hundred yards or so wide, each day, each mile, brought
another bend that opened up incredible new vistas of great
ice-hung black peaks, thousand-foot waterfalls, wild and sav
age tributary valleys reaching off on either side into the

Summer light lingers and dusts ice and clouds.

105

unknown. By the time we reached its confluence with the mighty Alsek, which cuts through one of the greatest mountain ranges of the world on its way to the Gulf of Alaska, our minds, hearts, souls, had merged and become one with the most powerful sense of wildness I have yet experienced in twenty-five years of wandering about the beautiful places of this earth.

That is why the Tatshenshini simply must be made safe, unmarred by any human activity except the transient passage of we who travel with it to the sea. That is why its potential fate—whether to preserve it or allow massive min-

106

Vibrant, iceberg blues are enhanced by overcast days, especially where recent calving has occurred.

A mellow beginning for rafters near the put-in for an Alsek river trip.

Guides treat guests to homemade ice cream created the traditional, hand-cranked way.

Rafters remain a safe distance from a hundred-foot wall of ice; a slab the size of an apartment tower could break off without warning.

Bob Herger

Kevin Schafer

ing—has so caught the attention of environmental communities in the United States and Canada, and has led to an unprecedented joint effort to protect it.

Desecration of this 2.5-million-acre wedge between the great wilderness complexes of the Wrangell-St. Elias-Kluane parks on the north and the Glacier Bay National Park complex on the south would be an act for which future generations could never forgive our own. If the wilderness of the Tatshenshini is breached here, it diminishes in equal measure the grandeur of the entire complex—north and south—that presently exists. The wild rush of the Tatshenshini is the heart of this great international wilderness.

That is why, when the call came, it was so easy for national organizations in the United States to join with their Canadian counterparts in the coalition to achieve preservation of this magnificent place. And that is why it was so easy, I suspect, for then-Senator, now-Vice President Albert Gore and numerous of his colleagues in the United States Congress to speak out so strongly in support.

The fate of the Tatshenshini has yet to be decided. I trust that the British Columbia government will also see the wisdom of protecting the Tatshenshini, for it is the wildlife and fisheries of both nations that are at stake. As we move increasingly towards global and continental cooperation in the areas of free trade, the environment and security, it is appropriate and natural to recognize that rivers on the grand scale of the Tatshenshini, and the projects that might threaten them, are beyond the "ownership" of just one nation. The living wildness that is the Tatshenshini is a treasure that should be passed on, so that all who come in the future can feel that magic connection with something ancient and powerful, something reaching far back in time. Tatshenshini is North America's wildest river. If we in Canada and the United States have to fight to keep it this way, we must—and we will.

Brock Evans

Brock Evans is vice president of National Issues with the National Audubon Society.

Graham Osborne

The chill of a rain-soaked day
can be offset by the ever-present
beauty of dwarf fireweed.

The color of the luxuriant coat
of the glacier bear permits
greater camouflage when the
bear wanders across glacial
moraines.

Their life cycle complete, the
bodies of dead salmon are food
for others in the chain.

109

Bob Herger

AN ESSENTIAL BEAUTY
Pierre Elliott Trudeau

Of all the changes that will come to Canada in the next generation, we must prevent any of a sort that will diminish the essential beauty of this country. For if that beauty is lost, or if that wilderness escapes, the very nature and character of this land will have passed beyond our grasp.

Pierre Elliott Trudeau served as Canada's prime minister for more than fifteen years.

A fiery sunset spreads across the water of the Tatshenshini River near Sediments Creek.

113

"Across the wall of the world,
A River sings a beautiful song. It says,
Come, rest here by my side."

ON THE PULSE OF MORNING
by
Dr. Maya Angelou

Uncertainty, *by Mark Hobson suggests a lonely vigil by a wolf searching the Tatshenshini River valley for another of its kind, a situation that must never come to pass.*

115

Jacques Andre has been playing with cameras since his eighth year, an interest that led to an honors degree in photography from Emily Carr College.

Published work includes photos in *B.C. The Time of Our Lives* and *Stein: The Way of the River* and in *Beautiful B.C.* and *Western Living* magazines. He now lives on Saltspring Island in B.C.

Jacques feels strongly that as British Columbians we are extremely fortunate to have such incredible, diverse wilderness at our doorstep. He believes that careful sustained use of second-growth forests and secondary manufacturing of wood products can lead to a near-perfect balance of forestry and recreational wilderness use.

Presently employed with Environment Canada Parks Service as a landscape artist and project manager, Liz Baker manages projects such as the environmental cleanup and rehabilitation of Lyell Island in South Moresby National Park Reserve in the Queen Charlotte Islands. As a river-raft guide, she spent many summers on the Kicking Horse River in B.C. and many others throughout North and Central America and Nepal. She feels none of these experiences, however, can quite match the uncompromising beauty of the Tatshenshini.

Erwin and Peggy Bauer are photographers and writers of travel, adventure and environmental subjects who have specialized in filming wildlife worldwide for over forty years. They are based in Paradise Valley, Montana.

Recent magazine credits include *National Geographic*, *Outdoor Life*, *Audubon*, *International Wildlife*, *Sierra* and *Nature Conservancy*. They have a dozen books currently in print and another, *Wild Africa*, in production. They have won awards for wildlife photography in national and international photographic competitions.

Mike Beedell is an environmental photographer, explorer, author and eco-tour operator. He has spent most of the last fifteen years documenting his journeys through wild places—from the North Pole to the wild rivers of Tasmania. Mike's life was changed dramatically in 1978 when he co-led a canoe journey down an Arctic wild river (the Coppermine) in Canada's Northwest Territories.

Mike had purchased his first camera a few months before this journey and so his career as a photographer evolved on the trip. The author/photographer of the book *The Magnetic North*, Mike's work is regularly published in magazines and books throughout the world.

Marc Bell studied forestry and ecology at the University of British Columbia and Yale University. He taught botany and environmental studies for thirty years at the University of Victoria, where his research focused on plant ecology and its relationship to forestry, mining and parks.

Marc retired early to play and to spend more time in the forest, where he feels at home. Between traveling the world and exploring back-country British Columbia with fly rod and canoe, he catches shrimp for his family and friends from the porch of his houseboat in Victoria harbor.

Rick Blacklaws is the creative director of Image West Photography. Specializing in scenic land-use photography, he travels extensively throughout rural British Columbia and the Yukon. His style usually incorporates human activity dwarfed within a landscape. He is currently working on a three-year project to interpret the natural and cultural resources of the Fraser River drainage photographically. He has attended the universities of Calgary and Alaska, as well as Simon Fraser University, and now lives in White Rock, B.C., with his wife, Carol, and three children.

Ric Careless is the executive director of Tatshenshini Wild and chairman of the Tatshenshini International network (representing over 50 of the leading North American conservation groups and their 10 million members), which has been working to preserve the Tatshenshini since its formation in 1991.

Ric has played a leadership role in wilderness preservation campaigns for the past twenty years and has succeeded in protecting ten major areas totaling over 3 million acres. He cofounded the Sierra Club in British Columbia and has worked as an environmental policy advisor to the provincial government.

In 1991 he was awarded Environmentalist of the Year by *Equinox* magazine, and in 1992, he was the first non-U.S. citizen to be named River Conservationist of the Year.

Tom Cassidy is the general counsel for American Rivers, North America's leading river conservation organization, and a director for their Federal Lands Program. Based in Washington, D.C., Tom has coordinated United States legislation efforts on behalf of the Tatshenshini. He joined American Rivers in 1989, and is involved in river conservation issues throughout the United States, developing particular expertise in Alaskan issues. In 1990, he and his wife, Joy, floated the Tatshenshini.

Before joining American Rivers, Tom was an attorney in private practice in Annapolis, Maryland. From 1979 to 1982, he was the Legislative Representative for the Mono Lake Committee in California.

Outdoor Photographer calls Carr Clifton "the most rapidly rising 4x5 star." A native Californian living near Taylorsville, he has spent many years exploring the wild places of North America with his view camera. He is best known for his contributions to the Sierra Club and Audubon wilderness calendars, and *Outside* and *Wilderness*. Carr's books include *California: Magnificent Wilderness; New*

CONTRIBUTORS

York: Images of the Landscape; The Hudson: A River That Flows Two Ways and *Wild By Law.*

Nick Didlick is currently a staff photographer with the *Vancouver Sun* in Vancouver, British Columbia. Born in England, Nick grew up in Maple Ridge, near Vancouver.

Nick has worked as a photojournalist with United Press Canada in Vancouver and Reuter News Pictures Service in Brussels, Belgium, and London, England.

Reuters nominated him twice for a Pulitzer award, and his photos have appeared in every major newspaper and magazine, including the *New York Times* and *Stern, Newsweek,* and *Vanity Fair.*

He returned to Vancouver during the summer of 1989 to enjoy the outdoor lifestyle the west coast offers. He rafted the Tatshenshini River during the fall of 1991.

Brian Dechene is a professional photographer who lives in Calgary, Alberta. Brian works in both landscape and portrait photography and is best known for his striking panoramic landscapes.

Michael Down is one of Canada's most accomplished mountaineers, with a lengthy record of technical first ascents on many of North America's greatest mountains, including Mt. Logan, Mt. McArthur and Mt. Fairweather in the Tatshenshini region. A longtime wilderness

advocate, he cofounded the University of British Columbia Enviromental Interest Group in 1980, and, most recently, served as president of Tatshenshini Wild. Formerly a professional mountain guide, he runs a sales agency representing several lines in the outdoor sporting goods business.

Peter Enticknap lives in Haines, Alaska, and is vice-chair of Tatshenshini International. He first became aware of proposed mine development in the Tatshenshini River valley in 1989 and began contacting Canadian activists for support. He has published numerous articles on the Tatshenshini and has traveled across the continent advocating protection for this remarkable wilderness area. He also serves on the board of the Southeast Alaska Conservation Council (SEACC).

After graduating from law school in the eastern United States, Brock Evans moved to Seattle, Washington, and promptly fell in love with the wilderness of the Northwest. He became active as a citizen volunteer in local environmental issues and was hired in 1967 by David Brower of the Sierra Club to cover a territory from Alaska to California, including British Columbia and the Yukon. Since 1973, he has acted as a top lobbyist, first for the Sierra Club and now for the National Audubon Society in Washington, D.C. Brock experienced the Tatshenshini in 1990.

An itinerant rafting and fishing guide, David Evans has been rafting around the world for ten years, the last four leading trips for Canadian Rivers Expeditions on the Tatshenshini. One of British Columbia's provincial rafting examiners, he is based in Smithers, B.C., where he guides steelhead fishermen for Farwest Steel-

head Lodges. He expresses his personal philosophy with these words. "I have come to terms with the future. Every day I walk easy on the Earth. Plant trees. Kill no living things. Live in harmony with all creatures. I restore the Earth where I am. Use no more of its resources than I need, listen to what it is telling me."

George Figdor is a photojournalist and publication designer who lives in Juneau and Haines, Alaska. He has spent a number of years photographing in the Chilkat Valley near Haines, and his photographs of the eagles and the valley ecosystem have appeared in several wildlife publications. He has also produced audio-visual programs about the Chilkat Valley. He is a past president and current member of the Haines-based Lynn Canal Conservation Organization.

Heather Hamilton's first loves are animals and the Earth. She became an ethologist and spent several years working for the National Museum of Nature, studying muskox and arctic hare behavior and ecology in the Canadian High Arctic. Currently she is conservation director for the Sierra Club of Canada. She also developed and coordinates the Sierra Club's Tatshenshini Biodiversity Field Research Program, undertaking ecological studies in the Tatshenshini-Alsek watershed. She lives near Ottawa, Ontario, with her husband, one horse, two dogs and five cats. In her spare time, she rides and trains horses, walks her dogs, and reads and writes murder mysteries.

Like many other photographers, Al Harvey's career is the result of a hobby that wouldn't stop growing. His collection of transparencies became the foundation of today's Slide Farm, a library of about a quarter-million slides that are used by an ever-growing clientele. The Slide Farm specializes in geographic themes around the world—the diversity of physical, economic, cultural and human geography. Outdoor and back-country photography remains a favorite theme. Other favorites include playing hockey, being immersed in tropical turquoise water, quaffing unpasteurized ale and discovering seafood buffets.

Bart Henderson has been guiding wilderness trips and photographing rivers and mountains around the world since 1969. His explorations have taken him to Africa, Asia, South America, Southeast Asia, islands in the Pacific, and the North American continent, including Alaska.

He organized and led the first guided trip on the Tatshenshini in 1976. Bart is the owner of Chilkat Guides, one of the oldest and largest rafting companies in Alaska. His photographs have been published in many books and magazines worldwide.

Bob Herger has spent years visiting and photographing the coastal region of British Columbia. His numerous books include the award-winning *Forests of British Columbia* and *The Coast of British Columbia*. Among his list of clients is Tourism BC. Bob rafted the Tatshenshini in 1991 and found it to be an overwhelming experience. He lives in Maple Ridge, B.C., with his wife and three daughters.

Stephen Herrero is a professor of Environmental Science and Biology at the University of Calgary, Alberta. Author of *Bear Attacks—Their Causes and Avoidance*, he has been deeply involved in bear studies and publications about bears for over twenty years. He is recognized throughout the world as a leading authority on bear ecology, behavior and attacks. He is currently cochairman of the IUCN/SSC Bear Specialist Group and is past-president of the International Association for Bear Research and Management. In the summer of 1992 he

headed a research team conducting preliminary studies on the conservation significance of bears in the Tatshenshini.

Mark Hobson is a painter and photographer whose work in both mediums has won international awards. Although best known for his West Coast images, his passion for wilderness and keen interest in natural history have drawn him to many remote corners of the world, including northern B.C. and the Yukon. He has donated the proceeds from the sale of prints of his painting, *Uncertainty*, to the cause of saving Tatshenshini.

Anne Holcroft-Weerstra is a freelance wildlife biologist based in the foothills west of Calgary, Alberta. She has spent several years conducting research on black and grizzly bears and their habitats in the Rocky Mountains and foothills of Alberta. She has also been involved in numerous other wildlife and botanical studies in western and northern Canada. In the summer of 1992 she was part of the research team conducting preliminary studies on the bears of the Tatshenshini River valley.

Based on nearly twenty-five years as a professional conservationist, Monte Hummel is now president of World Wildlife Fund Canada. He is author/editor of over 100 popular and journal articles, many book chapters, and three books, including the Canadian bestseller, *Endangered Species*. He has a particular interest in the conservation of large carnivores.

James Katz is the owner and director of James Henry River Journeys, a California-based company that has been operating educational trips down the Tatshenshini-Alsek rivers since 1978 and on western U.S. rivers since 1973. Katz has been on assignment for *National Geographic* in the Arctic,

and his work has been published in *Outside, Sierra, The Wilderness Society*, and other publications. He is also a photography instructor for UCSC and UCB Extensions and teaches courses at Pt. Reyes National Seashore in California. James lives in Bolinas, California, with his wife, Carol, and daughter, Danielle.

Specializing in outdoor adventure subjects, Jim Kay's home near Salt Lake City keeps him close to many of his favorite photo locations in the mountains and canyons of Utah. When not shooting near home, he travels the world on assignment or in pursuit of stock photos with his wife, Susan, who collaborates with him by writing articles. Jim's work has appeared in *Sierra, Outside, Islands, Ski, Nature Conservancy, Nikon World* and *Outdoor Photographer*. In pursuit of his commitment to the environment, Jim also donates his photographs and time to various environmental organizations.

Ian Kean's love of adventure has developed into a way of life. Seasonally, he enjoys plying the icy torrents of North America's wild rivers. He has instructed British Armed Forces in whitewater maneuvers on Alberta's mountain waterways, and most recently, he has guided raft expeditions on the Tatshenshini. Off the river, Ian lives a life according to conscience. Involving himself in endangered-species projects such as the Great Jasper woodland caribou study, Ian's latest endeavor brings him to the humanitarian field as a medical relief worker. He has spent time in the breakaway state of Croatia, and hopes to continue in this work.

Nature photography has taken Bill Keay and his wife and assistant, Wanda, on expeditions from Kenya to Canada's Arctic. His images are sought after by art collectors and have been presented to heads of state. His work has won awards,

including the Best of Canadian Bird Photography, and his book, *The Wild Life of Bill Keay*, is enjoying critical acclaim. Bill and Wanda live in Lions Bay, B.C., with their two daughters.

Robert Glenn Ketchum provided the American public with the first feature story on the Tatshenshini-Windy Craggy controversy, published in *LIFE* in May 1991. Author of *Overlooked in America: the Success and Failure of Federal Land Management; The Tongass: Alaska's Vanishing Rain Forest;* and *American Photographers and the National Parks*, Ketchum's career in photography has been distinguished by his success as an environmental activist, which has earned him the Ansel Adams Award for Conservation Photography, and the United Nations Outstanding Environmental Achievement Award.

Currently serving as curator of photography for the National Park Foundation in Washington, D.C., Ketchum's work is exhibited and collected worldwide.

Born in Vancouver, the youngest of eleven children, Andrew Klaver loves the back country. Through corporate and editorial photographic assignments he has traveled extensively around North America. But when he was asked to shoot images for a Canadian River Expeditions' Tatshenshini brochure, he jumped at the chance. It was a trip he will never forget.

Harvey Locke, president of the Canadian Parks and Wilderness Society, is an environmental lawyer living in Calgary. Harvey's photographs have been published in many publications, including *Canada: The Mountains, Borealis* magazine, and numerous calendars and newspapers. He has hiked and photographed in the Andes, the Alps, the

Himalayas and eastern North America. He spent twelve days on the Tatshenshini in July 1991, and has been heavily involved in the international effort to protect its wilderness.

Ken Madsen is a writer, photographer and outdoor educator living in Whitehorse, Yukon. He authored *Tatshenshini Wilderness Quest*, coauthored *Rivers of the Yukon—A Paddling Guide*, and his articles and photos have appeared in *Explore*, *River Runner*, *Currents* and *Canoe*. He has paddled throughout western North America, Mexico and New Zealand, including many "first descents" in Yukon, northern B.C. and Alaska. When he isn't exploring wilderness rivers, he is working for wilderness preservation as the president of the Whitehorse-based society, Friends of Yukon Rivers.

Starting with the classic Kodak Brownie, Tim Matheson has been making photographs for twenty-five years. Concentrating on work in the cultural and environmental fields, Tim's work has appeared in international magazines such as *Outside* and in many local publications. A strong involvement in multi-image production has seen his photographs featured in presentations at the Hong Kong Museum of History and the Banff Festival of Mountain Films. He is also involved with live performance, producing images that are projected as an element of the set design. He works with many of the principal theater companies in western Canada.

Johnny Mikes, owner and operator of Canadian River Expeditions, has spent many years in the Tatshenshini and Alsek watersheds. His love and concern for the Tatshenshini was the catalyst for the current campaign to preserve it as wilderness.

Johnny grew up on the rivers of western Canada and is one of Canada's most accomplished river runners. His expertise as an expedition leader and naturalist was gained on waterways ranging from the rivers of British Columbia, Alaska and the Yukon to the shores of the High Arctic and the Queen Charlotte Islands. He is currently writing a river-running and natural history guidebook to the Tatshenshini-Alsek.

Liz Mitten-Ryan is a Canadian wildlife artist renowned for her ability to give life to her art. As a concerned conservationist, her paintings have an educational value—Liz's wildlife is always captured on canvas in its environment.

Her powerful piece, titled *Commanding Presence*—a statuesque grizzly in its home territory of the Tatshenshini River—won her the B.C. Wildlife Federation Artist of the Year award for 1993.

Liz has studied at Heatherly's School of Fine Art in London, England, the University of British Columbia and with Peter Aspell. She paints from her home on the Sunshine Coast, which she shares with her husband, six children and an assortment of farm animals.

Pat Morrow has established a hard-won career in the often precarious business of adventure photography, writing and filmmaking. Together with his wife, Baiba, he has shared the complex planning and sometimes harrowing challenges of assignment work on the world's seven continents. They have documented their experiences in magazines, newspapers, books, multimedia presentations and, more recently, on film and video. The Morrows depend on the wild places they document to be pristine and have donated their work in support of preserving a number of threatened areas, such as the beautiful Tatshenshini.

Pat O'Hara's work takes him throughout western North America and abroad, photographing the natural environment. Pat pursued a master's degree in forest resources at the University of Washington, and has been working as a professional photographer since 1978. His images have appeared in hundreds of publications, including *American Photographer, Audubon, National Wildlife, Outside,* and *National Geographic,* as well as books, calendars, posters and advertisements. His list of credits also includes the Photography Gold Medal, awarded by the New York Art Directors Club, and *Communication Arts* magazine's Award of Excellence.

Pat, his wife, Trina, and daughter, Trisha, live in Port Angeles, Washington, where he works out of his studio on Mount Pleasant.

Since the 1950s, Rick O'Neill has ventured into many areas of photography, but his favorite has always been nature. His work has been featured in several magazines, including *Beautiful British Columbia, Westworld,* and *Earthkeeper,* as well as the book, *Songs from the Wild,* and many environmental publications.

He is a member of the Sierra Club, the Western Canada Wilderness Committee and the North West Wildlife Preservation Society . These and other organizations have used many of his slides.

A wide-ranging traveler, he has photographed in all provinces and territories of Canada, and throughout the United States, Mexico, the Caribbean and Europe.

Joe Ordonez is a naturalist, river guide, tour leader, photographer, writer and potential stand-up comic. He has been guiding river trips down the Tatshenshini and Alsek rivers since 1987, and he works as training director for Chilkat Guides river trips through the Chilkat Bald Eagle Preserve. His photographs and articles have appeared in the *Chilkat Valley News,* the Mountain Travel/Sobek catalogue and the book

122

Rhino, on the brink of extinction. Joe is founder, president and sole employee of the fledgling company Rainbow Glacier Adventures, in Haines, Alaska.

Graham Osborne is based out of Vancouver, British Columbia. Graduating from U.B.C. with his degree in wildlife biology, he now works full time as a photographer and journalist. Osborne specializes in large-format landscape, wildlife and outdoor photography, and has completed a coffee-table photographic book of the wilderness landscapes of B.C., published by Douglas and MacIntyre. Osborne's photographs have appeared in numerous publications, including *Canadian Geographic, Buzzworm, Photo Life* and Western Canada Wilderness Committee calendars, and he has worked on assignments for *Equinox, Beautiful B.C.,* and *Canadian Airlines.*

Sally Ranney, president of American Wildlands, has spent the last eighteen years in the field of wildland resource protection and management. She was appointed by President Reagan to serve on the United States Commission on Americans Outdoors, served as a resource policy analyst for the Wilderness Society, cofounded the World Congress on Eco-Tourism, and chairs the global Earth Restoration Alliance. An author-lecturer with degrees in education, geology and art, Ranney's commitment to the environment comes from a background in ranching, her experience as a former owner-manager of a rafting and adventure travel company, and a life-long love affair with the West, where she was born.

Bart Robinson is the editor of Equinox: *The Magazine of Canadian Discovery.* He currently lives in Sydenham, Ontario, with his wife, Susan, and son, Matthew. A strong wilderness advocate for the past twenty years, he has authored or co-authored a number of works on the western mountains, including the *Canadian Rockies Trail Guide,*

Great Days in the Rockies, and *A Solitude of Ice*. After refining his formula for a long and buoyant life— "look for wildflowers in the mornings; run whitewater in the afternoons"—on a trip down the Tatshenshini in the summer of 1992, he says it is transparently obvious that we should be "enshrining it, not mining it."

Kevin Schafer is a freelance wildlife and nature photographer who regularly travels to remote parts of the world from the Arctic to the Amazon and most places in between. He fulfilled a lifelong dream by floating the Tatshenshini in 1991, on a story assignment for *Audubon*. His work also appears in many other publications, including *National Geographic*, *Natural History*, *Outside*, *Sierra*, and *International Wildlife*. He currently lives in Seattle with his wife, Martha Hill, a well-known writer and wildlife art critic.

John Schnell is a resident of Springfield, Illinois, and has been photographing the Alaskan and Canadian wilderness for the past two summers, using a large-format camera. A love for adventure travel and wild places culminated in a whitewater rafting trip on the Tatshenshini River in 1991, and a subsequent trip on the Alsek River in 1992. John's images have recently been published in *Alaska*, and his corporate clients include IBM.

Raised in Alberta, Robert Semeniuk completed graduate school in Environmental Studies at York University, and photography workshops at the University of Kentucky and the Columbia School of Photojournalism in Missouri. Since becoming a photojournalist in 1978 he has worked in over forty-five countries, including Afghanistan, Burma, Punjab, Somalia and Tibet, and his photography and stories have appeared in numerous publications, including: *GEO* (Germany), *Gente Viaggi* (Italy), *Helsigin Sanomat* (Finland), *Equinox* (Canada), *National Geographic*, *Popular Photography*, *Time*, *Newsweek* and *Camera Arts*. He has won awards for his work and lives on Bowen Island, near Vancouver, British Columbia.

The executive director of conservation for the Canadian Parks and Wilderness Society, George Smith is working on conservation issues concerning the Tatshenshini, the northern Rockies and the Tetrahedron, and on a West Coast marine parks system. His past includes newspaper reporting, initiating a system of cabins and trails in the Coast Mountains, work with native political organizations, and federal government work with the office of energy conservation and the secretary of state. He lives in Gibsons, on the British Columbia coast, and his passions include back-country skiing, hiking, birding and canoeing.

Phil Timpany is a naturalist, professional photographer and videographer, and his keen sense of animal behavior lends a realistic perspective to his work. A lifelong interest in wildlife and wilderness has led him into many remote corners of the Northwest. Living in Atlin, B.C., he is actively involved in video production and stock footage sales through his company, Wild Eye Productions.

Edgar Wayburn graduated *summa cum laude* from the University of Georgia and *cum laude* from Harvard Medical School. He pursued an active career in medicine, both in the private practice of internal medicine and as a teacher at Stanford Medical School.

His second vocation as a conservation activist brought him to the presidency of the Sierra Club of the United States for five years in the 1960s. He has served on its board of directors almost continually since 1957. He initiated and led three of the United States' major conservation campaigns—for Redwood National Park, Golden Gate National Recreation Area and the Alaska National Interest Lands Conservation Act. He is currently Sierra Club vice president, as well as chairman of the Alaska Task Force.

Art Wolfe is a celebrated wildlife/ nature photographer, famous for his revealing portraits of wildlife. He capitalizes on an animal's distinguishing features, natural behavior and habitat to capture an insightful, at times humorous, glimpse into the creature's private world.

Art works on assignment and publishes frequently with periodicals such as *National Geographic*, *National Wildlife*, *Smithsonian*, *GEO*, *Audubon*, *Time*, *Life*, *Esquire*, and the *New York Times*. Art has also released a video, *On Location with Art Wolfe*, filmed in Alaska's Denali National Park and Kenai Peninsula, and has participated in Kodak's educational program, *Techniques of the Masters*.

Photo Credits

Photo of Ric Careless by Pat Morrow
Photo of Carr Clifton by Kathy Clay
Photo of Brian Dechene by Harvey Locke
Photo of Michael Down by Sharon Down
Photo of Dave Evans by Bob Herger
Photo of Mark Hobson by Lorna Walsh
Photo of Robert Glenn Ketchum by Amy Holm
Photo of Tim Matheson by Jane Bartlett
Photo of Johnny Mikes by Mark Hobson
Photo of Pat O'Hara by Tina Smith-O'Hara
Photo of Sally Ranney by Judie Brown
Photo of Kevin Schafer by Wayne Lynch

Front cover image by Kevin Schafer

Permissions

Bart Henderson

A rainbow adds a cap of color to a fortress of ice on Alsek Lake.

125

Kevin Schafer

Art Wolfe

Art Wolfe

126

John Schnell

Kevin Schafer

Art Wolfe

George Figdor

127

United Stated Publishing Data

International Standard Book Numbers:
        1 - 56579 - 040 - 5 (clothbound)
        1 - 56579 - 041 - 3 (paperback)

Library of Congress Catalog Card # 93-60595

Production Credits

Executive Producer: Ken Budd
Designer: Ken Budd
Design Assistants: Rory Christianson
        Dawn Faulkner & Michael Tiernan
Photo Editors: Ken Budd & Bob Herger
Text Editors: Ric Careless, Ken Budd
        & Johnny Mikes
Copy Editor: Elaine Jones
Color Separator, Printer & Binder:
        Wellrich Pte. Ltd.

Publisher & Distributor

WESTCLIFFE
PUBLISHERS

Westcliffe Publishers Inc.
2650 South Zuni Street,
Englewood, Colorado 80110
Phone: (303) 935-0900
Fax: (303) 935-0903

Producer

SummerWild Productions
#2202 1275 Pacific Street,
Vancouver, B.C. V6E 1T6
Phone & Fax: (604) 681-0015

Printed on recycled paper.
Printed in Singapore.